salmonpoetry40

Publishing Irish & International Poetry Since 1981

MORE PRAISE FOR UNSAFE

"There is warmth and light, darkness and danger in these poems. O'Kane drops anchor into the pedestrian moments of the everyday and creates a unique mosaic of domestic vignettes that often take us by surprise."

Mel McMahon

Raw and emotive, O'Kane's work is driven by the power of memory, channelling both nostalgia and melancholy with pinpoint accuracy. These distilled micropoems and lyrically complex lengthier pieces are vivid and ultimately rewarding. A brave and uncompromising debut.

Ross Thompson

Geraldine's poems tell of memories that are silently screaming, here they have found a voice where she is urgently reporting back as a witness. She speaks of trauma and the resilience that comes over time. She is Hitting to Hurt, I feel in an effort to heal us; she says "This is the room where I last saw you." and she certainly sees us, she unflinchingly looks to meet your eye and then devastates us with all it means to be utterly human.

Stephen James Smith

Unsafe

Geraldine O'Kane

Published in 2021 by
Salmon Poetry
Cliffs of Moher, County Clare, Ireland
Website: www.salmonpoetry.com
Email: info@salmonpoetry.com

ISBN 978-1-912561-40-7

Cover Image:
"The Lady Vanishes" by Brian Kielt
Oil and Charcoal on Canvas
© Brian Kielt
www.ungalleried.com
www.briankielt.com

Cover Design & Typesetting: *Siobhán Hutson Jeanotte*

Printed in Ireland by Sprint Print

The publisher gratefully acknowledges the support of The Arts Council of Ireland / An Chomhairle Ealaíon

The author acknowledges the kind support of the Arts Council of Northern Ireland through their Artist Careers Enhancement Scheme, and the Support for the Individual Artist Programme

For Mum and Dad

"when your mind breaks the spirit of your soul"

21 Guns — Green Day

"I've let my emotions out the hive again"

Crossroad — Artan

Acknowledgements

Some of these poems have appeared in the following publications and anthologies: *Ascent Aspiration, Black Cat Poems, Community Arts Partnership anthologies Still, Moments and Connections, Flare Magazine, FourXFour Poetry Journal, The Galway Review, Lagan Press Online, The Lake Poetry Journal, Message in a Bottle, Oddball Magazine, Poems in Profile, Poethead, Windows: Irish Women Write Poetry*, and *Her Other Language*.

'Stark' was chosen by Judge Luke Kennard for the *50 Best British and Irish Poets Anthology 201*7 by Eyewear Publishing. 'Reading' was shortlisted and 'Matthew's Shop' was commended by judge Leontia Flynn in the 2016 Glebe House Poetry Competition. 'Burying Boys' and 'Hitting to Hurt' were commissioned by artist Brian Kielt for an exhibition in partnership with StART Talking, shown at the Duncairn Arts Centre, March 2015.

Heartfelt thanks go out to the following encouragers: my husband, best friend and partner in poetry, Colin Dardis; Mum; Dad, nieces and nephews Rebecca, Roisin and Rachel, Michaela, Paddy, Tom, Mick and Emmett, they mean the world to me. In no particular order, but in equal merit: Brian Bailey (RIP), Keith Acheson, all the sttaff at the Crescent Arts Centre, Deirdre Cartmill, Olive Broderick, Maria McManus, Lynda Tavakoli, Bill Jeffrey, Peter Francis Fahy, Azeem Lateef, Will Donnelly, David Yates, Elizabeth McGeown, Stephen Gordon, Mel McMahon, Susan Millar DuMars and Kevin Higgins, Ruth Carr, Eliz Byrne McCullough, Chris Ledger (RIP), Colin Hassard, Chris McLaughlin, Siobhan and Peter McCafferty, Anne Marie Mullan, Ray Givans, Paul Jeffcut, Brian Kielt, Tory Campbell, Amy Louise Wyatt and Paul Rafferty, Stephen James Smith, David Braziel, Ross Thompson, Chelley McLear, Alan Hayes and Damian Smyth – thank you for your support and honesty.

Thank you to all who have become friends and supported me through our monthly Purely Poetry open mic poetry night. Thank you to the Arts Council of Northern Ireland for financial support, encouragement and an unending belief that my poetry was worth pursuing.

Contents

Places

after 'I Come From' by Orfhlaith Foyle

I come from
a lineage of forked tongued women with strong backs
mixed with odd, spirited, laid back men.
I come from
the blood of the Easter Rising
James Connolly shed for Ireland;
I am a creative recipient of the vein.
I come from
the mouth of every browbeater,
a complex translation of their lexicon.
I come from
yuppie parents hustled from their marriage;
back then you didn't talk of mental health.
I come from
Yeats's widening gyres,
stronger for proving the centre can hold.
I come from
the college sick bay to find out *What Katy Did.*
I come from
God, more powerful than an electric current,
a drop of love in the world's ocean.
I come from
the priest who pushed me down in the playground
because he could.
I come from the scars on my knees.
I come
flat packed, open,
ready to be built each dawn.
I come from
thirteen teenage bedrooms,
the single teddy-bear Santa left for my tenth Christmas.
I come from
pre-birth photo memories of grand men,
grandmothers gone before I knew the women behind the titles.

I come from
words and books
and the only book I've read more than once,
The Time Traveller's Wife.
I can close my eyes, hear
ga-gun-dadak-dadak, ga-gun-dadak-dadak,
your heart wood-pecking your chest,
legs extend and flex, feet find the right bounce,
no thoughts, just survival.
My back tells me running is where I came from.
I can still time travel with you,
ga-gun-dadak-dadak.

While I Remember

i.

When you become smaller
than birth, there is much less
to pick on.

ii.

The epicentre
of the divorce,
I was their shrapnel.

iii.

Children who pecked at me, as men
became friends of my father, the bar
tender.

vi.

Gooseberry jam is Granny in a jar;
when I need faith, I open the lid,
breathe her in.

The Ordinary Life

for Mum

You were *May*
but when you arrived
with your suitcase
at the back of our bungalow
I knew it was summer.
Colours exploded out of the suitcase
when you flipped those brass fasteners,
materials soft enough to pass any face test,
everything for the taking.

I remember a tablecloth red pinafore
with yellow flowers and rope straps.
I wore it with no t-shirt and white sandals that year,
the same year my sister covered herself in cooking oil
and fell asleep on our sun lounger.

I played in the back field, the fauna tickling at my face
and made imaginary tea, while you sat dark-haired and swarthy
on a deck chair, in matching short-sleeved blouse, ankle length skirt
and open toe sandals, knitting cardigans and talking with the neighbours.

May must have been the death of you each summer,
she could have been your sister-in-law.
I wonder if she ever spoke his name to you, told you of his life?
My memory made you ordinary; cocktailed with yours,
added a storey of strength not found in any fairy tale.

Then We Were Four

for baby Mary

You pop up in daydreams,
night dreams and meditations;
as a child, my guardian angel, a teenager.
Lately you are a twenty-something with glasses,
long almost-black hair, looking like
all three of us, jaw a little longer, squarer.

Sometimes I think you Godlike,
we will never see the face of you — our sister.
Some day we will all be gods.

The Couple

after Philip Levine's 'The Two'

The black and white haze
of strangers caught in a moment
on a random park bench
reminds me of bony stories
I cannot put flesh on.

You got married
in a place I have never visited,
yet I have seen you both
in chromatic photos
together smiling out at me;
shapes I have only ever known
as separate entities.

I heard you spent your honeymoon
on a park bench in Edinburgh,
you were happy then;
how bad must things have become.

When Memories Awaken a Fire

As you entered our bungalow a right turn
took you past two bedroom doors
to my favourite room,
at the end of the hallway,

a fifty pence meter hung above its alcove.

I remember my father lifting me
up past his shoulders to insert the coin,
turn the knob a whole half way.

My only brush with magic,
making the light reappear.

Known only as the 'green room'
in summer it became a forest,
paint flecks turning into shadow trees
as my voices echoed back to me.
It was cold, damp crept the walls.
My eight Barbies, one Ken and ragdoll Nelly
wrapped up warm for daily wedding and tea parties.

The house, a renovated cottage,
kept intact the large windowsills.
I was too young then to realise
they would have made perfect
window seats for reading;
instead I curled up habitually,
used my toilet roll telescope
to look out on Lough Neagh,
silent keeper of its fishermen.

Playtime

We were playing hide and seek round our estate /
when he grabbed my wrist.
Much older than the other kids,
he would know all the good places, so we ran...

He took me to the best spot,
"Scream," he said,
"no one will hear you."

Stark

You tell me over breakfast
your husband raped you.
I set down my cup
to look past your face
at shoulders protecting your heart.
"What do you want to do about it?"
"Nothing," you confirm twice.
I finish getting ready, leave for work.

In the car I run words, images back and forth:
had I misheard anything, was there something amiss?
The white lines come close, disappear.
I pull over, breathe, pound the steering wheel,
embrace it, lay my head there for a second,
breathe, pull out again.

Later I call you to see how you are.
You assure me that's not what you said,
"It never happened, no, it never happened."
I let it go, but I've never forgotten.

Therapy

She doesn't like couches
especially leather ones;
siesta beyond your welcome
and experience the loathsome /
peeling/of exposed skin
akin to the slow rip of a Band Aid
to reveal an unhealed wound

Vivid
met.
Sound.
peel

and yet here she is
stretched full length, legs crossed at the ankles;
a hypnotic voice urges from a cavernous beard:
take me back — slowly from the compartment of her mind
she pulls the memory, unfurls it
like a ruby red rug, follows the path
to the death of her childhood.

Rug met.

It's 4 p.m. when she realises you are late,
the uniformed laughter of the bus stop
turns caustic in her ears; quietly she slips
from the group to the phone box sanctuary.
Lifts the receiver, she connects to conjoined sobs.
Without a word she hangs up, dials three little digits
for an operator to inform her an ambulance is on its way.
Exiting to the low groan of late afternoon traffic,
the entire universe seems to be suddenly packed
into her school satchel and pulls down on her shoulders.
Realising she is only a mile from her home
she begins to run but knows the battle is over
before it has begun; blue flashing wails
come in waves, then halt, envelop her.
Looking round she sees the paramedic
motion for her to climb in; like a failed criminal
she is known to them.

?
✓
Clunky
(But simulates 'official voice')
o - a
Maudlin met'
o
~ Cliché
,,
Sim
I o
Guilt.

20

They arrive at her home to find it locked up, blinds down;
breaking in is like waking a sleeping child —
soft screams seep from the shattered window.

Entombed in the ambulance, her mother
reaches out to hands folded near her naval
as if searching for an umbilical defibrillator
she can attach to her chest and restart
her petrified heart, as tear-swollen lips slur
"I didn't want to die today."
The daughter's inner child screams "neither did I,"
but outwardly smiles "it's okay, everything will be ok".

[handwritten annotations: "met. Medical.", "Cliché", "'Death of her childhood'"]

[handwritten note at bottom: "— NB Never use 'suddenly'."]

[handwritten top margin: Contrast, Comforting images, Tea. Food. Cats. Granny.]

The Living Room

[handwritten beside title: Rhythm. Simple & Sensuous.]

for Granny Canavan

[handwritten left margin: met / Ab. Weak]

My grandmother's kitchen was a tea cosy,
knowledge and love brewed there in equal measure.
Everyone reached full flavour inside that room —
with the softest unsliced bread in Ardboe
and the sweetest bananas.

The cake mixer was always whipping up something
to go with the tin kettle permanently on the boil.
If you were lucky you would hit on licking-time:

[handwritten left margin: Sound]

buttercream from the bowl is best! Days clinked
to a start, and ended with spoons stirring hot milk
and bread for her cats. She smoked twenty a day
in that room with hardly a window open and

[handwritten left margin: Smell.]

forever smelt of Yardley — *Lily of the Valley.*

[handwritten left margin: Stilted.]

Evenings rendered the kitchen silent
as everyone poured into the living room.

This Morning

At 5 a.m. this morning
I know you were a toasted marshmallow,
melted under the covers in pink pyjamas
with black dots. Your hair,
a sprawling arch across the pillow,
fizzy with static as it always is.

But now I am on the plane.

I realise if I were never to see you again,
this image would never hold up
for I never saw you,
I gave you no last look,
"have a safe trip" or "see you soon",
just "goodbye".

Clothes!
Details.

myth.

Nadelah

Pre-boundaries and pre-colonisation, I was *Nadelah* to
my Native American tribe, a sacred gift, a two
spirited, third gender, in continuous state of
transformation. Born raw, I existed ungendered until
the ceremony of the *basket and the bow*, where my
choice let me live revered not feared. Pre-boundaries
and pre-colonisation, I transcended the masculine and
feminine, to see in both directions. I was a conduit to
the spirit world, I lived a life of community, unaware
of my sexuality, until the white man straightened the
circle I inhabited. Renamed me *Berdache* — but I tell
you I was slave, sexual or otherwise, to no one.

Biligaana must show himself
a liar or conceive —
I am his single spectre.

Nadelah: one who has been transformed
Berdache: boy kept as sexual slave
Biligaana: Navajo for White Man

Deadly Games

She is ahead of the game, safe in the knowledge
he couldn't lift her by the ankles as he had proposed.
She isn't prepared for him to pull her to the edge
of the bed; burying her legs in the crook of his elbows,
like delivering a calf from its mother, beginning to swing
her around; renting a nervous giggle, closely followed
by an excited half scream, normally found lingering
at fairground rides.
                                 He swings faster and she seems
to be floating; an up and down movement, like beating
water with a foraged stick. Suddenly he loses his footing
from the circle, steps back for balance, hears a soft *thwap*
as her humbug head, pale and dark, connects
with the edge of the bed. Her giggles stop; body goes heavy
and limp, pulling at his arms. He lifts her head
from the awkward angle, takes her face in his hands
and waits for her to stop playing dead.

Tree Tunnel

for Colin

We walked mid-road under the tunnel of trees,
huge trunks branched above us,
their leaves feather boas floating
from about their necks, sheltered us for a moment
— only a moment.

In a split second through the arc of recess
where the sun had warmed to our skin
came sheeting rain; energetic beads
with bellies full, readily dropping their payload.

Adj

We did not twist in circles
with arms flung wide and heads thrown back,
catching rain with our open mouths.
After twenty minutes and two cars passing,
we were drenched, chills crept over our bodies.

We stopped, sought sanctuary along the verge,
you mimicking the tree trunks,
providing as much shelter as your frame would allow,
curling in on me, latent, against your chest,
chin resting on my porous hair;
elemental, I attuned to the call
of your heartrate, your skin…

when a car pulled over,
sweeping us away
from the summer downpour.

On Writing...

One half of me and my other half,
you are a physical magnetism, tangible, a brutal energy.

You are every colour
and the great mind that discovered the
therapeutic nature of the spectrum.

You are maple pecan plait
pulling ribbons of moisture from my lips.

You are pearls cold around my neck,
on my cardigan, skitter scattering
along the wooden floor.

You are the monster I have given in to.

You are Asclepius botching memories,
trying to shock them from my past
into my present life.

You are every face of my mother
except the smiling one —
that I shelve for myself.

You are festering in my gut,
spluttering out from internal places,
pulling the hearth of me with you.

You are an inherited banshee
screeching for status.

You are a caged lion tracking
back and forth just beyond the glass.

You are a selfie taken in the wrong light,
from the wrong angle.

You are what happens;
when I martyr myself
on today's tabula rasa.

Reading

We don't read the same books anymore.
I look at the young brown haired girls
on the cover of yours, say aloud, "that looks good."
You agree, "it's a great read."

You haven't yet encountered *the* bookshelf,
filled with my infinitely expanding *to-be-reads*
alphabetically and chronologically coded
by author then date of publication.
You and I never needed a system:
we just read, our memories agile.

I recall the summer we moved into No. 6:
it was hot enough to remove men from their shirts,
every front lawn became a beer garden,
dogs lay full stretch on shaded tarmac,
every day we ate *Magnum* ice creams.

On four chairs — two for our bottoms,
two for our legs — we devoured Maeve Binchy novels.
Our back garden became a settlement of
make believe characters; the sun cradled us —
the village gossips — as we laughed and cried,
passing stories and theories long after
we had pitched our bookmarks, lifted our chairs,
still trying to settle them into our new home.
I don't recollect another summer like it.

Left for Dead

Good morning, good morning!
I hear your phone chirrup in my ear,
the only part of me responding yet.
I know it's Saturday; I catch sound of you clattering
downstairs making wakey-wakey-eggs-and-bacy!

I rest the small pill in my palm
knowing, once inside, it will extend fingers,
pull all my limbs into balance.

I think of the poem half written
left for dead in my coat pocket,
words wrinkled like we've spent
a lifetime together —
uninvited meditations.

Into the car and under the bridge,
a blue-white checked blur toddles out,
brakes are hit, father reaches for thread of hood,
our eyes set on each other in expectation of lessons.

Deep into the countryside I find you on a hillock,
slender, bulbous with bald branches,
bearing the eight a.m. sunrise
high as an Olympic torch.

Spending Time

As it should be and feels like it always has,
we splay on our settee in the dinette.

You with laptop on your knee,
me immersed in words with legs curled up,
maybe a toe touching your thigh.

Sometimes there is music or radio,
oftentimes not — even our own breaths dare
not disturb this wholly natural scene.

Burying Boys

after the painting 'Form an Orderly Queue' by Brian Kielt

We stood around but
the waiting wasn't long,
bodies came quick one
after another, we soon began
to bury en masse.

At the start we were precious,
took every detail and belonging,
a half mercy to send home to families
along with *the news*.

Now we telegraph name, date of death, condolences.
Yet still we tried for that day we carried *news*,
the next it could be our names making their way home.

I never imagined when I answered
my *calling*, I would be preparing boys to die,
teaching them not to fear,
blessing their unmarked graves with foreign earth.

Only the dead have seen the end of war.*

* Quote from 'Soliloquies of England' by George Santyana

The Boss

We didn't meet by chance in the airport lobby.
She sensed in my obvious lack of eye contact
a pollen trail of discomfort and made a bee-line
in my direction to land an interrogatory enquiry
as to where on earth was I off to?
"New York," I replied to my own reflection,
trapped in the sunglasses perched like a tiara
on the perfectly coiffured crown of her head.

She was actually taken aback by my reply
as if my words had tried to steal her lunch money.
Recoiling, her pursed lips emitted a winded rebuke,
"You seem too quiet to go there."

The predictable employee-boss pleasantries
carried on, unabated, as she ignored
the confusion leaping from my stung face.
Should I discard my figure hugging jeans,
ditch my casual vest top and blazer?
Don an anorak and oversized horned-rimmed glasses
and go stand awkwardly in the background
of some stranger's photos?

On second thoughts, I remember I've already
applied my insect repellent, so sod her,
I'm off to America.
Yes, sod her, I'm off to America,
so excited I just had to say it twice.

Impeccable

He eases through the door into her line
of vision, without making eye contact.
The interior of their faces change to mirror
each other, as waning moon reflects on water.

He makes a seemingly off-the-cuff
remark about skiving; too quickly she reveals
she is running late for her engagement.
Their feet fall to a familiar silence.

She ponders the definition of their friendship;
they speak freely in many formats during the course of any week.
She doesn't do this with her oldest friends. Do the boundaries
of friendship lie within the ease of their conversations?

The moment is broken, he fills the hush
by pointing to that scratch on the paintwork — again.
They lean in close, heads bent, to inspect
if it indeed has grown visible; they make eye contact.

Poet Inherits the Fiddler's Left Hand

When I acquired you, I felt you got a raw deal.
Your musical days cut short
before you had time to perfect your craft.
For twenty years you were stretched on a daily basis,
just getting into the stride of retaining memory flexes.

Here you are, with me, making no more use of you
than to strain saucepans of water
carry full cups without spillage
help loop a lace or pull on a shoe.
You are infantile to this varied working life
I hold little hope you will one day
pick up a pen to tell your own story.

Plain as the rest of me, I allow you no decoration,
no sign saying 'look and adore me!'
More I encourage you
to work at your relationships
by staying unclasped, upturned, inviting.

You slide nail of forefinger over skin of thumb
mimicking a familial trait;
I see it as a nervous kneading and rolling,
a worrisome jealousy of the right hand —
the one I have spent my time with —
forging a strength you will never be capable of —
writing out the best of me.

The right hand has my memories running
rich through its sinew, earning the potential
to seek out its mirror image,
its comforter, its companion,
become entangled in its embrace.

You will always be a lightweight,
a bantam, a fingerling,
too little to love.

Definitions

Perched on a hospital bed opposite a doctor
resting easy in the high back visitor's chair,
he hands you a clipboard and paper, having drawn
a simple square, asking "Can you copy the shape for me please?"

You contemplate the pen he gives you
like it was just plucked from the back of a crow.
You always had beautiful handwriting;
I tried often but could not mimic its soft cadence.

Concentration lines take shape on your face
as you try to comprehend how you might
make the pen move on the paper.
Eventually you mark the page with a barely perceptible squiggle,
present it back to the doctor with a triumphant confusion.
Unsure if what you have done is correct but the relief
of your shoulders from having produced something defines the moment.

I want to enfold you in an embrace,
transfuse back into you all the knowledge
you poured into me from my very first breath
but you aren't finished giving, so I meet your eye,
smile and proclaim "well done".

Hitting to Hurt

Everybody saw us
as the bull and the lamb,
that is how I hid for so long.

He was a chunk of a man;
I sliced him to bits with my words,
buried him with shame.

I am sorry for using such callous language.
I'll try to reign myself in,
let's just start again.

The first time my hands rose it felt
like they belonged to someone else.
Afterwards, I wished so hard that they did.

It's not like it was commonplace
but the second and third time — I knew
the fists were mine and I kept on using them.

He stood there as I threatened to leave him
if he didn't fight back or if he did I'd go anyway.
Soon I was saving all my energy and hitting to hurt.

Once, I drew blood, no longer saw him
as bull, husband or human being;
then I knew I needed help.

Benburb Priory

Benburb was never home to us
but a passing mention of the townland
smoked out a memory
playing reveal and conceal with me,
leading to the question:
How did we end up in that unsettling room?

With storage heaters that made the space
feel like an ice box at night, stifling in the morning —
forcing us out of the worn bed
to wash immodestly at the sink provided.

A single file corridor with claustrophobic floral carpet
matching wallpaper and a 60 watt bulb
lead to *that* room where even our shadows wouldn't follow us.

Sitting in my sister's kitchen, a previous 5 a.m.,
shaken and sleepless: it was decided *that* room
would be the safest place for us;
now home was an abandoned word.

Just past midnight we had flipped and flitted
into the car in our pyjamas.
Panic quickly set in, as we snuck and groped for keys
foreign to the touch in our unlit hallway.
Senses found with the sound of the axe's
first strike against our back door —
step-*father* caterwauling,
"It's the last time you'll fucking call me an alcoholic,
I'll do time for you both!"

One word took me back —
to the women's shelter
to the night I'd misplaced.

Self-Sculptress

I prefer to think of you as 'Girl in Hat Contemplating'.
I dare not linger on the eyes piercing the fourth wall,
that tell me they wish they were blue as a sun bearing sky
inking the whole earth below it, signing its name on the lips
which beckon me close to whisper, "I wish I were fuller, majestic,"
before I feel the air around me being taken — long breath is drawn
into the nose in the hope that breathing-holding-letting-go will erode
extra membrane, bone and tendon, leaving something willow-like.
Sad self-sculptress hiding under hat and black baggy jumper
gazing at self in mirror; that is the terror I feel in myself
when I look at you, really look at you.

Head Binder

If I could blindfold you
I'd cut your hair to your nape,
puff it out with a back comb,
sweep your fringe off to the side,
let it soften the wilderness in your eyes.

I'd paint your lips matt bubble gum,
lather them with a high finish gloss,
let your spirit jolt with the pleasure
of every compliment received.

I'd become a surgeon: ease the squint
that comes with your every human interaction.
I'd under-crank your muscles just at the shoulder,
leave you elastic as exhausted lovers.

I'd hold a fish bowl to your mouth,
collect all your words, spill them straight
onto your notebook; your hand still a crude
translator of your mind.

I'd make you listen to others through your gut,
fetch them from strength and pitch of their language
instead of tacking flat words on their shoulders.

If I had a blindfold, I'd probably bind myself.

Portrait: Constructing Chaos

A living breathing Dali
brought to life's stage,
you are carefully constructed chaos.

Vixen of the worst kind;
chameleon without intent,
sucking colour from lives
onto your canvas.
Fuchsia lips a megaphone for
the Holy Ghost, smiling, always smiling
so no-one can see your cleft tongue.

Your wedding band obscured
by six inch stilettos, reveals
the temptress you are.

Cutting edge bangs
conceals untainted skin,
a smoke screen against peer envy;
insidious to those too anorexic
to play your game.

Giggling your way through conversations,
intelligence carried around
in your many pockets
a concealed weapon.

You masquerade hungry
for life, your canvass growing
more colourful.

How will you know
when you are truly satisfied?

The Great Compression

My body has become your lair.
Feasting on my energy, you feed,
become strong, lick at battle wounds barely healed
from our last encounter. Panther black,
crouched and ready for attack, you creep
towards my mind.

I know you have arrived
when you insert your animal head
perfectly inside mine, one creak
of your neck locking us in for the ride.

When I look through your feral eyes
the world becomes sepia
and I believe I can see above and beyond
everything into nothing.

Momentous

He stops talking, reaches out
with his writing hand, brushing skin,
and knows when he cups her face
it will paint a chapbook of words.
Their world becomes a kaleidoscope
of elephants on stork legs
as their lips meet;

his tongue firm and masterful
swipes inside her mouth
like a paw, playful with desire.
their bodies heave and resettle
with the heaviness of stoked coals
in a fire already burning.

Vulnerability Before the Storm

Up on her tip toes, she leant into him and kissed!
There was a gentle *schwa-p squidge* sound,
his eyes flicked open to see her unpeel
the canvas of the world, fold it up
neatly and place it in his breast pocket,
before turning to walk away.

The elements spread
through his body,
wet and warm.

Mama Bird

We slipped you from your intoxicating habitat
when your inebriated head bobbed and dipped the other way.

Clipped the wings that drove you —
your get-away from unwinnable situations.

We caged and tagged you so we could
love you at ease from afar.

How could we have still expected you to sing?

Room

This is the room where we sat
hands wrapped around mugs
of tea, mouths bound to your lemon
drizzle cake and town talk,
never breaching boundaries of ourselves.
Where we spun stories and tying the threads together,
found we were cousins as well as friends.

This is the room where I received
my first hug from a familial stranger,
my hard frame pressed against your flesh:
fingers testing a white pan loaf for freshness,
you were just out of the oven, warm to the core.

This is the room where we checked ourselves
in the mirror one last time, hair all strands in place,
lipstick on straight, you made me one of the girls.

This is the room we found him pacing /
hyped up more than usual, an animal snarling
"Where the fuck were you?"
"I said on the phone the child was sick."
You, crying on instinct,
"We left as soon as you called, where is he?
What have you done with him?"

This is the room where I, welded
to your kitchen doorframe, watched you hold
your baby boy like a shield about your face
as blows battered your fresh bread skin,
amid screams of "No, daddy, no, stop."

This is the room I returned to,
found you a blooming rainbow of bruises
bawling into the quiet; your son wrapped
tight to your chest.

This is the room where your family
found you on the edge of broken.
I knew they'd take you home,
try to love you back to freshness.

This is the room where, dropped on one knee,
you accepted him for better or worse,
for as long as you both would live.

This is the room where I last saw you.

Statistician

/ The alarm harries him from sleep. /
Routinely he rises goes to the window,
emits a little peep, "Snow!"

Unprovoked he showers, eats breakfast,
contemplates kissing his wife
but she works hard, deserves the rest —
he will return later with a plethora of lip touches.

On the dual carriageway his are the first tyres
to lose tread on black ice,
his hands first to brace the steering wheel
calculating stop distance, probable outcomes.
A panic rises from his ribs, he retreats to a safe place:
back beside his wife, he pecks her once.

Cuffed

Neck cuffed flat to the panel of our staircase,
between the curve of his thumb and fingers;
he is twice/my age/and the same/in height.
His figure comes towards my mouth
takes away all the light, I shake my head,
try to get loose.

Earlier he had stooped, peeped
his silhouette through our back door,
where I stood alone in our narrow kitchen.
He took a step inside, stretched out his palm
revealing two glistening bullets,
"For your stepfather," he said, "you choose which one."

I shook my head and slipped
back to our New Year's Eve party without a word,
thinking how they looked too dense to fly,
too blunt to tear through sinew, skin and bone.

I'm still squirming as mum sidles merrily to our front door
having delivered each neighbour home with a hearty goodnight,
she has always been kind like that.

Coming into the light of our porch her smile sweeps
through to angered comprehension,
"Get your hands off my daughter."
One step and a swoop of her fist knocked him clear.
It's not the first time my mother's hands rose to champion me.

Noose

He used to greet her with a noose,
wait for her to 'talk him down'
until the sight had her turning on her heel;

voice squeezing through the closing
front door "do it, see if I care!"
Unsure if she believed.

Poet

Without you there is a world
with a place in it for me;

a nook not part of my being,
that says 'put on your galoshes
and pirouette for me,
pretty ballerina.'

The Eye of Time

The earring sat at the last step of the stairwell
where they used to kiss voraciously
after days of being apart.

Unsure of when it got there,
she didn't dwell on it,
but they did eyeball each other
from time to time.

The pearl offered its own explanations:
maybe it occupied the carpet
before her feet ever tread there;
perhaps it belonged to the previous tenant-
men vacuum regularly in a man's way-
for there it remained long after they left
and their love died.

Months later she visited his bed,
laid naked in emotions,
when there in the rumpled sheets
stared back at her the earring
accompanied with a hair;
this time it was less placid,
told her straight: they had more right
to be there than she did.

Another Dawn

Dawns are often heart-breaking,
I watch you with panther eyes
for the slight up and down movement
of quilt, as a mother lingers
at the doorway of a sleeping child.

It is not solace or comfort I look for,
more a daily justification for leaving you.
Your invisible judge and jury will always find me;
guilty, but cannot forever hang me
in your gaudy scenes of still life.

Authoress Envy

She lives the lifestyle:
goes to parties
where music is strummed
on acoustic guitar
to red-wine-infused audiences perched on
soft sofas, flickering in tea-light ambience.

Wears penniless chic
from second-hand stores,
her pale pallor hiding
feisty undertones
hinted at by vixen-red lips
and earthen hair draping her waist,
a throwback to free love.

Her last home,
some stranger's floor;
at 3 a.m., what stories it told.

It's not her words I envy:
it's a life that soaks onto the page.

Satú's Song

I was born under the lullaby of quetzal,
god of the air, and for the privilege
was protected by an amulet made in its image.
I grew strong, no wound ever fissured my skin,
I was pure, my people respected me.

My uncle, ready,
stole into my room and away with my amulet.
My uncle, ready for the throne,
speared me from a distance.
My uncle, ready for the throne at any cost,
burned my bloody remains on the forest floor.

The quetzal came, imbibed my essence,
sang of my passing a sacrifice
so I could return to the mountains.
Only true Boruca knew
I was 'god of the air' all along.

In Costa Rican folklore the Queztal was protector of Satú chief
of the Boruca tribe. When killed by his uncle, the quetzal took
Satú's spirit to live in the mountains.

Van Gogh's Chair

Citrus and lime colours
attribute your contentment
to a point.

Then your pipe laid down,
a gift to the chair
that embraced your stagnant
body when no one else could get close.

Culture Dogs

We lap up culture from the space between talk,
letting our tongues wag out poems —
overheated dogs.

We honour the word
by bringing it to the people,
assembling them in huddles
with comfortable seats.

We are the mud and wattle holding
tradition together,
protecting literature —
bringing it forth on a platter.

We are the message made visible
within the full lipped smiles of those
who open their hearts
and let us graffiti them with beauty.

The Couple

They sleep in separate bedrooms,
dream in parallel
worlds,

chaffing

at each other's
edges.

Majestic

No one knew you were a stilt walker, it just sort of happened,
no one saw you lumber around while you found your feet.
Just, one day people started to look up to you,
even when you weren't doing anything.

You've been up there so long,
spent so much time breathing a different atmosphere,
you have become tainted by your own reality.

Some have mistaken this detachment
for majestic gracefulness and wisdom,
have taken to calling you *swan* and *princess*;
but your hair has never grown long enough
to let others scale your heights and get to know you.

When you are that high up, you become stilted,
unable to move within the lives of those who try to love you.

Charlie Sings the Blues

I don't care
if you have found a sitter,
the first time out
after months of sleepless nights.
Your post-natal bump
tells more than you'd have hoped.

Sipping your drink,
so it doesn't go straight to your head,
is not working.

Really it's that kind of goings on,
hands and tongues, snakes devouring,
that got you in this state to begin with
and if you're going to go there again,
get a room or a dark alley.
Leave me to my strawberry daiquiri
with two straws.

Effect is the Word

after Seamus Heaney's 'Mid-Term Break'

On the outset, his choice: create or never create again.
Challenged, he stared into the lily-white void,
bricked it up with an army of inky black words

using isochronic images carved from his own eyes
that said: stay with me, discover my depths;
I will tell you no lies, for it is what it is,
there is nothing more behind.

As she left her world to journey
through twenty-two lines of his,
a rabble of butterflies gathered on her skin
forming a mosaic montage of mourning;
every hair on her body responded
in raised waves of salutation,

while with synthetic synchronicity,
a solitary tear sluiced from her
and splattered onto his words:
a four-foot box, a foot for every year.
In perfect recognition of the moment
a *poppy bruise* appears: beautiful and harmless,
like the beat of a butterfly's wing
changing both their lives forever.

The Dangers of Internet Friending

1.

I knew a man whose name was Shakespeare.
To be honest I had my doubts,
he didn't really write in that particular
poetic phrasing.

When I say knew,
what I mean was we had more
of a to-ing and fro-ing engagement
of words over social networks.

He had a humour big and bold
as his exclamation marks!
What wasn't there to trust
in those winky smiley faces?!

Until one of them turned up
magnified,
a plump red berry in my peep hole
unannounced.

2.

You and I have been friends
online for some time;
today I found you thought
I was someone you knew.
For my part — I am one
who likes to see the tick
of people's minds.

You sent me an audio olive branch,
your latest experimental music montage
with lots of synthesisers and autotune.

I typed back it was awful good,
my brain only agreed with one
of those words,

but you couldn't see my face
so we are still friends
online.

Plant this Poem

Plant these words, firmly in your frontal lobe.
Nourish them gently until the roots take hold
when your busy day is done let their poetical rhythm
meander methodically through your mind in meditation
massaging your temples as they go.

Let them be a lullaby,
luring you through the lucid labyrinth of slumber,
in the morning becoming the larcenist of your dreams.

Irish Weavers

We weave our tongues through
crude intricacies using definite words:
'the Troubles' and 'poetry'.
Mid-flow I am distracted
by a kamikaze leaf
skimming shadow from
the building opposite.
I point it out to you.
We let its spiralling
silence us into autumn.

Boy Next Door

Standing in the local chip shop, nothing fancy
just the usual set-up, utensils and owner encased
behind one of those burglar-proof high-rise
counters, and me taking up floor space
on the other side, looking at the ice cream;
there is always an ice cream counter taunting —
You are having chips but you could have me!
Go on have me now, you'll be finished
by time the chips are ready, it'll be our little secret.
I was still deliberating when you strolled in.

All at once the room became small
like a three piece breaded chicken box,
me a drumstick shoved in the corner;
the air started to do yoga poses
whilst trying to jam itself inside my mouth and lungs.

You and I made eye contact,
the awkward kind like the quick heavy pull
of a fish taking the bait, discarding of the need
for usual, mundane pleasantries.

As if the situation couldn't become any more intense
on the TV screen in the corner appears
the mother of the man you are accused of killing.
The volume was turned down but all three of us saw it,
her face, magnified, as if we were all squished
through the same looking glass.

You made your excuses and left,
as you walked away I was struck
by my own moral compass.
In my eyes you will always be
the boy next door, who I kicked football
with and sang stupid childish songs.
I'm having trouble relabelling you
as suspect, accomplice, murderer.

Voyeur

(after 'Girl Powdering Her Neck', Kitagawa Utamaro, c. 1790)

All his features point up towards her
on the pedestal of his desire,
eyes squinting under the opulent glare
of her creamy nape, her open flesh
Pavlov's bell.

Her svelte fingers linger just long enough,
the way Victorian hems were designed
to ride up baring half an inch of ankle,
just a tease

before gliding up to let loose an avalanche
of ebony hair that will silhouette her body
in all the right ways, leaving him exposed
to her will.

Captivated

If you were a book
you'd be a lithe novella;
not crowded with words
but meaty enough to hold all *Watchers*
Captivated.

Cloaked and bound in red leather
You'd be soft to the touch,
indestructible under the *Reign of Fire,*
hinting at a penchant for danger.

Times New Roman would be your default font
with quotes emblazoned in bold italic,
tattooed into the minds of your lovers,
to be used after you have *Gone with the Wind*
to the *Empire of the Rising Sun.*

You would start out as the epitome of a sprawling family drama,
descending into a coming of age,
would follow a red brick road
so no one could see the bloody destruction left in your wake
as you *Push* on, destination unknown.

Critics would try to compare you to *Murphy* or *The Dumb Waiter.*
Unperturbed by labels, you'd busy yourself
disputing the authority of *Warhol's Prophecy.*
Magical realism would lure you from reality,
your slight of word would become so natural
even Banville would spontaneously combust in spectacular technicolour
akin to a catherine wheel nailed to *Birchwood.*

You would be a first edition, a second and a third
yet you would never be a classic,
trending on every social media site
for your infamous banning in the interests of public safety;
it will be said the poetic beauty of your words
drove readers to the brink.

You would be a reference point,
every man's blog roll,
more than *A Heartbreaking Work of Staggering Genius*.
Even the most hardened sceptics
would weep between your pages,
for they too know *No One Here Gets Out Alive*.

Object

There is no shame in tenderness,
so rip the cross binding your mouth,
perform a verbal striptease that leaves
aghast and agape the barren makers of the muse.
Caress their egos with your silken tongues
and give praise to the men who immortalised us
as sexless and sexy seducers of their patriarchal power,
who founded us as goddesses of love, war and the home,
depicted us as mothers of country, earth and children.
We grew, iridescent in their adoration —
carnivalesque felines with no howl.

This is our time, to slash open the chambers
and meaty sinew of the secret keepers
who have been innovators and captivators for centuries.
Abandon your halos, slip into a cotton dress,
feel confident in your own fleshy chic.
Cut up your power suits and lay down your stilettos
used as modern day spears
to stab the hearts and backs of men.

Breathe deep and expunge forth your fiery vocals;
take them as your muse, for all men are not broken,
as all women are not devoid of sound.

Portrait IV

"Who opens the curtains in my room?"

"I do, when you get up."
Dark rooms are infused with sadness, I inform you.

Two of us dwell in this house,
both living in the half shadows of half-truths.

What I really want to say is:
this pitch black room is a physical representation
of what you have become.
I open the curtains in hope;
the heat of nature's sunlight will stream
a heal-all army into you.

Resuscitate your petrified heart,
shrivel the cobwebs in your conscious,
unclamp the life sucking demons attached to your bones.

Instead I wish you goodnight, the ritual complete.

Printmaking, Typesetting and the Space between Words

Four small wooden blocks,
centuries old, probably,
defunct lettershop press.

Intricate I silk-screened,
marbled and block printed,
finally I sorted metal and wood type
into words.

Every white space between every word —
an object.
A printer has to think about negative space
                as something tangible.

En Space — rectangular metal or wood
whose primary purpose is to be smaller.
It is never seen, it doesn't catch ink,
doesn't sit proud, not an ordinary character,
nonsense, a trick, a flourish, a dingbat.
Printing is as much an act of spacing
as an act of marking.

Inefficiency is a virtue in a print workshop,
spaces in the composition —
spaces in the workplace.

It doesn't take a turtleneck
to see why
                blank space

                is moving.

An impure found poem from an article by Lindsay Lynch, 'How I
Came to Love En Space'. published in theatlantic.com, Sept 9, 2016

Weekday Poem

Monday's poem slow to rise,
is not a child at all,
still hibernating under the blanket of Sunday night,
has restless legs, desperately itching to kick through
the rest of the week, is peeking over Tuesday's shoulder,
eager to see what comes next.

Tuesday's poem shrugs off Monday's poem,
already overcome with dramas, dalliances
and disappointments, all sugar-coated into one.
Feeling much longer than it should be,
too many verbs and not enough full stops.

Wednesday's poem is a teasing army of sleep
marching past lunchtime eyes
under a cloud of addled optimism —
almost over or only halfway there.
No longer looking like a poem,
more a dog-eared note strewn in the corner
awaiting the recycle bin.

Thursday's poem is intense,
taking no shit from anyone,
for there isn't time for that craic;
is egotistical, declaring if you've lost your noetics,
intensity max or general originality,
then remove yourself from the poetry arena!

Friday's poem starts off with more of a whistle
than a bang, holding in the id for maximum effect later.
Finds itself lagging behind with googly eyes
far bigger than its social belly,
is tucked up and sober by half ten.

Saturday's poem is the horizon achieved:
head cocked, resting on its elbow,
looking out at the kaleidoscopic world
with compound eyes;
is over indulgent, insatiable,
drunk on life and saying yes to adventure!

Sunday's poem wants to stay up late,
sucking at the sap of enjoyment
like it may never return; is multi-dimensional,
at once a sleeping child, death a memory box
tucked in, stowed away, sleeping peacefully,
a genuine reflection.

Sunday's poem is a sacrilegious fusion
where dark and light get spliced,
creating an ambiguous equilibrium of energy.

Mouth

I know you
by the scent of your words.

Your porcupine coat
prickling playfully between us.

Your tongue flares on my horizon,
our days and nights become
illuminated.

Your name a daily grace,
a salutation, a lament —
hear my call.

Lip locked our barbarous tongues alight,
making our own fire —
survival.

Ducklettes

Sun settling behind trees,
ducks asleep mid lake,
no coaxing with crumbs
will tease them from dreams.

*

Ducklings scatter and re-scatter
as the hen weaves, bobs, resurfaces,
repeats,
teaching them water ways.

*

Our hands absent of bread,
ducks still tread to water's edge,
sleek, majestic, glistening
with humble dominance
of their home ground.
They find kinship in you.

Unmotherly Nature

Time does not fancy itself as a feminist:
so when this particular topic tapeworms itself
into conversations, I am glad to see
none of my friends have fallen victim to vanity fads,
for we are entering that age
when the hands of our body clocks are fondling
the strings of our frontal lobes.

? mixed metk.

More often now, I'm launched
into my own version of Hamlet,
arrows slinging from throats;
you are not a mother, when are you going to be,
that is the always the question.
With my answer — no, these hips hollow of maternal marrow
were never meant to yield children —
comes the crease of forehead and crouch of brows,
sumos squat, engaging each other before battle.

string - l
Strong l metk.
Stilted .
? Violence.

My words a sour sherbet gift
spat into their little "o" shaped lips,
yet they never ask why, so I never regurgitate my empty words:
I am not a follower of Eve, food is not my drug
or if they were inclined to climb my family tree
they'd find fruit littering every branch,
viral long before the die back ash tree saga.

Clunky.

My tongue has become a sword in this charade,
delivering the show stopping line: — *Cliché*
"But I want to adopt when I'm older,
give a child a chance to be loved."
Former truth is now my trump card;
when played, I watch the interior of their faces soften,
raise their fertile eyes to meet mine.
Time is no misanthrope but humans are diehard.

Sword met. violent-
Cliché.

Arresting. Trans adj.

76

Restless

It's been over six months since I last left
the heavy reality of my concrete world behind,

breathing in the earthen scent,
allowing hills to roll —
bolster my heart against my city tarred chest.

As I pass the place where my Granny rests,
I make/the sign/of the cross;
for though I have lapsed, found my own path
— label me as you will —
I cannot displease her, even in sleep.

I know who owns every plot of land I pass,
salute every face as a magpie,
for you never know who'll be
for the worrying these days.
Yet this is not my home.

Home is you, the day I took you down the one car road,
sandwiched between fields, past the shebeen
to see The Old Cross; let you rest your poet's palm
on its mortar; survey the stump
where the wishing tree used to shelter graves.

We walked across the chapel grounds,
looked over the lough, shimmering grey
as it does even on the brightest of days.

Just when I feared your illusion was dispelled,
there below us on a grassy knoll,
a white cow grazed with its herd.

Later we left that narrow road for home
with open hearts and wild eyes.

The Goblet

You were shiny once:
that is how my parents found you,
glistening at a sun soaked outdoor market.

Obviously you weren't new
or they would never have been attracted.
It was your scuffs and scars that drew them in,
the fascination of your untold history;
if you'd had lips they wouldn't have let you speak.

The wonderment of your squat stature,
your intricate stem
coupled with your lack of kin,
forced them to take you home,
give you pride of place

in the living room's dark ochre cabinet
where future hands could never reach.

But that was before:
before children,
before divorce,
before when scouting for shiny abandoned

objects together was a source of joy.

Now you look old:
mildew has dulled your exterior,
you have begun to break down;
I think you will have to go back in the box.

Matthews' Shop

Summer days spent with cousins holding tea parties
inside the tractor tire steadying the whirly line,
making tree houses and hedge tunnels.
Exhausted, we would clench our twenty pence
pieces tight in our palms as we headed to Matthews' shop
for Tip Tops, Ice Pops, a Joker if it was a scorcher
and my favourite, the 10p mix up.
If we were lucky enough to be collecting granny's pension,
that would earn us each another thirty pieces of silver.
My treasure was chocolate ice cups, their coloured foils
catching the light. After removing their ribbed cups,
there was chocolate tastier than Nutella from the jar.
Sweeter than slipping into pyjamas just after school,
superior to your team scoring a goal in the championship!

Mrs Matthews opened and closed
the post office-cum-shop at the same time each day.
She ran a snug establishment, no children beyond the counter top — ever!
A shrewd eyed older lady in pink two-piece cardigan,
grey below the knee skirt, imitating her cropped hair.
Never in my time did I manage an extra flump
or penny chew: if one ever strayed into the paper bag
it was instantaneously plucked to the safety of its container.
Someone must have been thinking about all those saved penny chews,
one day Mrs Matthews was mugged whilst closing
the steel shutters on the shop front.
She never darkened the door of her shop again.
Selfishly, I thought of it as a robbery of childhoods still to come.

Unsafe

Just myself on a milk crate, I play some jazz on my mobile phone, imagine myself knee sliding past the walls *he* just had painted Magnolia, *breathe* to complement *his* Egg Shell floor tiles, *breathe* to contrast with the dark mahogany of his windows, *breathe*. The hard wearing Oatmeal and Chocolate rug came half price with his Navajo Ivory leather suite, *breathe*. The Bronzed lady with the Muted Mustard headdress looks sadly at me, from the frame *he* put her in, *breathe*. I look off into his kitchen and see a desert of Sandstone tile and Natural Linen units, all *his* choosing, *breathe* a clean look. I try to warm the room with my fuchsia dress as I wait for *him* and the delivery men.

A canary has
fourteen breaths
to find a mine unsafe

Mother of all Migraines

No matter where it migrates to,
the seedling always forms in the temples.

Wriggling until it reaches
its home of nourishment;
imbibing fluid from the spinal canal,
spindly roots take hold,
expand out to ribs and beyond.
Soft, ripe shoots attach to retinas,
burst a bloom of rainbow around eyes.

Scents beelike,
honey and vipp around the nose,
trying to pollinate the entire body.

A gang of blacksmith strikers
forge an upside down horseshoe,
their deep *thungs* gush molten sparks,
just inside the scalp, burned and branded.

In the end velvet tones become caterwauls
as I deny the sun and everyone my face;
creativity springs with every pulsing blow
and I try to remember the last time
this gothic horror lead to aesthetic expression.

My Faux Angora Fur Hat

You were serene as a blanket covering ears;
as feet disturbing first drift of snow;
as a barricade of eyes against first blush of light.

A comfort-muffler to the background of my day —
hum of radiator, harmonising with breath;
rumble of kettle rocked by its boiling;
pit-a-pat-trickle-plop of rain on hood;
bleep of mouth at beep of horn;
chirrup and buzz of uninvited calls, birdsong;
unfailing reverberation of overhead planes,
rustle, sniffle, achoo — restless shuffling before bed.
You were a tea cosy for the sun
aping midnight with a round diamante brooch
giving luminous shift to mohair threads.
You could have been a pair of Ragdolls
curved into each other upon my head,
ruched elastic; snug against my nape
ouroboros — a tail.
Your peak lifted my face higher than Tibet,
took me past Everest, it was like God held a hand
close to my mind fashioning a static charge of creativity
every time you bedizened my head.

On Sofas

Huddled under blankets;
soother of the temporarily sick.
A magnetic force,
drawing the metallic hangover taste from your mouth.
Witness to cuddles;
unspeakable intimacy.
Guardian of any time weeping space,
confidant of ice cream, crisp and chocolate binges.
Infinite landscape when alone,
extension of yourself.
First big item fought over
then bought as a couple.
Red hot on cold nights
pulled up with your feet in the fire.
Mother of the living room,
lounging in the hallway,
a treat in the kitchen,
easy to get into, the devil to get out of!
Scratching post,
show of wealth,
squeaking, sagging, squishy,
thread bare,
abandoned in alleyways.
Thrown over, covered, re-covered —
family time.

Venus in my Living Room

I was wearing the creativity bracelet you bought me,
the night that Venus and Mars were visible alongside the moon,
and a girl wanted to sing *Strange Fruit* to the President Elect.

The same night a butterfly came into our living room,
and a single speck of glitter was caught hanging
on the coat tail of a cobweb —
twirling, visible and wondrous.

A Fiction

Six years my granny's senior, you were her best friend.
I remember you just as you are in this photo:
jet white hair, short set curled to your scalp,
soft crying eyes and a gentle curve of the mouth.
You used to take your glasses off to wipe away tears of laughter.
Like an old Indian Chief, your face had an abundance of lines:
merriment lines, lines of mischief running under your eyes,
smoking lines bracketed your mouth when you weren't smiling,
worry lines from the eight children you brought into this world,
'you left me too soon, my love' lines.

In the photo you wear a knitted jumper, plain,
a knee length nylon skirt plain,
a single plain gold wedding ring.
It doesn't show but I know you wear brogues black,
knee high stockings, that always showed long bloomers
when your body fell back against the sofa with a slap of your thigh!
People of your generation understood the need to ceilidh for the craic,
a quiet escape from the hardship of a young widow's life.

Not all feminists shouted from their pedestals,
born during the suffrage movement.

I read the inscription you were seventy-seven when you passed
which made me eleven in nineteen ninety two;
how well I remember a fiction of you.

Moon Mother

If they ask, "looking past you,
to the moon gearing itself for
the night ahead; showering in
the setting rays of the sun
just behind your head."

Not looking at the vintage handbag
tethered to your neck by a friend,
its handle short, leaving it to rest
on your full-bodied chest as a giant necklace.
Nor the blue blanket with the white stars
adorning your knee, already beaded with rain,
another kindness.

I am staring past the pink rain sheet
and coffee-to-go mug in your good steering hand.
I am boring right into your centre,
to the place your courage lives,
cupping my hands for scraps, for I know *You.*

I have helped unstick your wheelchair
from disability unfriendly places.
Have listened to your creativity wiggle
its way beyond your paraphernalia.
I have witnessed you arriving and departing
in a flurry of unabashed inconvenience.

I have never asked your name
or anyone else's, in case my enquiry
be misconstrued as a hand of friendship,
that is the length of my courage.
I will say, "I was looking at the grace of the moon."

Making Eggs

Omelettes for breakfast!
As I turn to agree you are already breaking eggs into a bowl,
the most natural thing in the world,
trusting your hand to separate yoke from white:
balance you say is important, two on one.

I'm ten years old, standing at the cooker with her.
Her red hair flaming in Saturday sunlight,
we are making omelettes as we always do:
ham, mushroom, cheese, tomatoes (on her side only).
Three summers from then, she will leave me without warning
and I will stop knowing how to break eggs.

Your voice pulls me back
to our kitchen, our life.
I have loved relearning with you.

Devotions

I pulled back from the urge then learned not to caress;
he wasn't that kind of man.
After the children we went to separate bedrooms.
We put on an amalgamated show for Mass and what-not special occasions,
we'd smile, laugh even; the odd time he'd uniformly reach for my hand.
I expressed affection by the room full — flowery curtains, ornate furniture,
inch deep carpets, soft shimmery wallpaper, hearty cooking,
scouring the house spotless, by the time our children arrived the house
was teeming; a smothering bouquet of unused love.

When the kids were small we moved from country to town,
he did his back in and I gave up driving, not to be contrary you see;
it left me up and out of the house to clients before dawn and home to
    make his tea.
We'd sit in the living room together communicate via *the* news and
    programmes.
Local talebearers bestowed a martyrdom on me —
'look at him indoors while she's out on the road swelter or snow'.

Then it happened, he got sick.
The first time I entered his room I barely recognised the shrivelled man,
stood in front of me. When I reached to take off his pyjama top I was
saddened to see loose flesh where muscles once resided — as a builder he'd
    had big beefy arms.
I found a pigeon chest nesting where his pecs used to be.
When I ran the cream over his parchment skin with my own work-a-day hands
I was afraid I would shatter him.

I got to know the stranger in the room; the slow curve of his collar bone,
the rigid terrain of his flat shoulders, the small rough patch in his stubble.
I found in me a devotion I didn't know I was capable of, for this body
who asked nothing of mine in return.

A Gift for You

Only you and I know that once
I bought you a caged bird; back then
neither of us knew what the gesture meant.

The lady at the pet shop said "no refund"
but I was sure, as you stood on the plateau
of new retirement, still of stimulation
and voices, this bird would bolster time
you could no longer 'work' to fill.

I knocked on your door, said,
"Remember those love birds you used to have?"
Before you could answer, I thrust
the responsibility of that little life
into yours; "Auk, she is beautiful," you said,
but you had lost too much.
She had to go back to the shop.

Today, I brought you a gift,
free of cages, my words wrapped
in an everlasting voice,
a poem for you.

GERALDINE O'KANE is a poet, creative writing facilitator and mental health advocate. Her work has been published in numerous anthologies, journals and zines in Ireland, the UK and the US, as well as appearing in Arlen House's anthology of new women's poetry from Ireland, *Washing Windows? Irish Women Write Poetry, Her Other Language.*

She is one half of Poetry NI, a multimedia platform offering opportunities and resources for poets in Northern Ireland.

Geraldine has given a TED Talk for TEDx Belfast, and read at the Poems Upstairs Series in association with Poetry Ireland. She was recipient of the Artist Career Enhancement Scheme '15/'16 from Arts Council of Northern Ireland, and one of Eyewear's Best New British & Irish Poets 2017. Her poems have been listed in the Melita Hume Prize, and Glebe House Harmony Trust poetry competition. She won the NW heat of the 2013 All Ireland Poetry Slam and represented Ulster in the final.

Her micro poetry pamphlet *Quick Succession* was published by Pen Points Press in 2014.

Geraldine is co-host and regular reader at the Purely Poetry open mic nights in Belfast. She has also curated two multi-platform exhibitions (Poetic Perspective and Product of Perception).

She is currently supported by Arts Council NI, the Big Lottery Fund, and the University of Atypical. She is working towards her second collection and on a YA play set in 90s Northern Ireland.

salmonpoetry

Cliffs of Moher, County Clare, Ireland

"Like the sea-run Steelhead salmon that thrashes upstream to its spawning ground, then instead of dying, returns to the sea—Salmon Poetry Press brings precious cargo to both Ireland and America in the poetry it publishes, then carries that select work to its readership against incalculable odds."

TESS GALLAGHER

The Salmon Bookshop
& Literary Centre

Ennistymon, County Clare, Ireland